WHAT IS SPIRITUALISM?

AN ADDRESS

DELIVERED BEFORE THE

Society of Spiritualists,

AT PENNY'S HALL,

IN THE CITY OF EAST SAGINAW, MICH., ON THE CELEBRATION OF THEIR

TWENTY-THIRD ANNIVERSARY.

ALSO, A SUBSEQUENT ADDRESS

DELIVERED AT THE SAME PLACE, ON THE QUESTION OF

WHAT BENEFIT IS SPIRITUALISM TO MAN.

By GEO. A. LATHROP, M. D.

Published by Request.

EAST SAGINAW, MICH.:

DAILY COURIER BOOK AND JOB OFFICE, OPP. EVERETT HOUSE.

1871.

WHAT IS SPIRITUALISM?

AN ADDRESS

DELIVERED BEFORE THE

Society of Spiritualists,

AT PENNY'S HALL,

IN THE CITY OF EAST SAGINAW, MICH., ON THE CELEBRATION OF THEIR

TWENTY-THIRD ANNIVERSARY.

ALSO, A SUBSEQUENT ADDRESS

DELIVERED AT THE SAME PLACE, ON THE QUESTION OF

WHAT BENEFIT IS SPIRITUALISM TO MAN.

By GEO. A. LATHROP, M. D.

Published by Request.

EAST SAGINAW, MICH.:

DAILY COURIER BOOK AND JOB OFFICE, OPP. EVERETT HOUSE.

1871.

A CARD.

East Saginaw, Mich., April 12th, 1871.

Dr. Geo. A. Lathrop—

Dear Sir:—Earnest in the cause of truth, and grateful to our loved ones gone before, for the *positive knowledge* of our immortality, we are desirous that other inquiring minds shall have every encouragement in their efforts to attain a like knowledge.

Believing that your very able addresses before the Society of Spiritualists, at the recent anniversary, and on a subsequent occasion, will be conducive to this end, we respectfully ask of you a copy of the manuscripts for publication

A. Farnsworth,	A. B. Spinney,
L. C. Whiting,	William Baker,
W. Paine,	F. F. Gardner,
A. K. Penny,	M. A. Root, Bay City,
Seth Willey,	Sanford M. Green, "

East Saginaw, Mich., April 13th, 1871.

To Messrs. A. Farnsworth, L. C. Whiting, M. A. Root, Sanford M. Green, W. Paine, and others.

Gentlemen:—It affords me great pleasure to learn that the hastily prepared addresses which I delivered before the Society of Spiritualists in this city on their twenty-third anniversary, proved acceptable to you, and I shall be pleased in accordance with your request to furnish you the same for publication, if, in your opinion, it will tend in any degree to make our views better understood and to afford to the materialist, evidence, and to our christian friends more rational and satisfactory grounds for belief in the immortality of the soul, as it will thus accomplish the object for which it was intended.

I am, gentlemen, yours with great respect,

GEO. A. LATHROP.

WHAT IS SPIRITUALISM?

LADIES AND GENTLEMEN:—This day being the anniversary of the advent of Modern Spiritualism, or more properly the day when for the for the first time attention was so directed to the subject that by following up the feeble suggestions then received, the key was discovered which solved the mysteries and gave to the world an intelligent comprehension of what they had previously regarded either as superstitution, or belonging to the domain of that in which many retained a lingering belief, and denominated sorcery or witchcraft: I have considered it appropriate to the present occasion to answer the question which is so often propounded by the opponents of our philosophy, viz.: What is Spiritualism? By some the question is asked in their ignorance of the subject and with an honest desire, and for the purpose of learning the truth; but by others in a spirit of affected and contemptuous scorn, and to give expression to their malice and hate. These latter often expose their ignorance of the subject by attempting to reply to the question themselves. "Oh," say they, "but we know all about it. Spiritualism is rapping upon tables, and moving them through the tricks of the so-called mediums, or by the aid of electricity, or galvanism, or magnetism, or odic force, or the will power of the medium upon matter, or the devil, or else the persons so believing are physchologized and made to believe as real, that which has no existence except in their excited and diseased imaginations." All spontaneous exhibitions of spirit presence or power are accounted for by them on the ground of hallucination, or as the result of the operations of a diseased mind. These are the answers of those who have but slightly, if at all, investigated the subject, and who have never made themselves familiar with the literature of spiritualism or the grounds on which a belief in it is based, or whose minds are so warped by their previous prejudices, that they are incapable of dispassionately weighing the evidences which spiritualism furnishes of its truth; and often will they wrap themselves in their ignorance and prejudice, and refuse to let in the light, for fear that what their spiritual guides tell them, is true, *viz.:* that it is the devil attempting to lead them astray. But the enlightened spiritualist listens to these puerile chidings and misrepresentations, with feelings of pity akin to contempt, for those whose narrow minded prejudices and bigotry have prevented them from listening to facts and reason, and prejudging and condemning a cause with which they are almost totally unacquainted.

But the answer which the intelligent spiritualist would give, when taken in its broadest sense, is, that spiritualism is the science of the soul. By science we mean the result of that accumulation and recorded observation of facts, by which we have been able to work out and elucidate those great laws which are the basis of and underlie all truths, and which enable us to understand their modes of manifestation and action. In our investigation of all scientific evidence, we start with this great axiomatic truth, which needs no attempt to demonstrate it, as it is intuitively recognized by the mind, *viz.:* that all phenomena in nature, or, in other words, all effects, are the result of causes operating for their production, and not the blind and fortuitous results of chance. In other words the belief of the spiritualist is an intelligent, scientific belief, founded on evidence, and the result of his reasoning, and deductions on comparison of the vast accumulation of facts which have come under his observation, while on the other hand the so-called christian claims that his belief is not the result of evidence which he has received, but is with him purely a matter of faith. His faith, he tells us, is "the evidence of things not seen—the substance of things hoped for;" while the faith of the spiritualist is the evidence of things seen, felt and heard, and the substance of things (not hoped for) but known. He knows whereof he believes, and instead of going back to the misty records of two and four thousand years for evidence founded on the dim and uncertain relation of what is reported as having occurred in ages long past, and which has to many minds failed, to carry conviction of its truth, he at once seizes upon that which he sees with his own eyes, and hears with his own ears, evidence which he knows to be reliable, and which when weighed and examined in a spirit of candor, rarely fail to carry conviction of its truth to the mind.

The charge is often brought against spiritualists by the so-called christian world, that their ranks are largely filled from the non-christian part of community—from the infidels and atheists. So said the Jews of old to Christ, because he instructed the publicans and sinners; but he, with keenest satire, replied; "I came not to call the righteous, but sinners to repentence." And I would say to such, while you claim to have sufficient evidence to convince you of the immortality of the soul, will you deny to those who cannot accept your belief, and embrace your hopes, the only evidence that will convince them, that the brief life we live here does not terminate with the dissolution of the physical body, but that we continue as intelligent beings, expanding in knowledge and progressing in wisdom and goodness forever.

The disbelievers in the immortality of the soul are not such from choice, but because sufficient evidence has not been presented to their minds to convince them of its truth. No man can control his belief. The mind unfettered intuitively yields to evidence, and the greater weight of evidence even as the greater motive, will always govern. How often the materialist replies to us: We hope it may be so, that physical death is not the end of life; but we have no evidence of it, and we have accepted the cold and cheerless belief in annihilation, not from choice but from an irresistible conviction of its truth. And oh! what a source of joy it has been to such when the facts of our philosophy have been made known to them, and its evidence has carried conviction of its truth to their minds; and then instead of looking upon death as an eternal separation from those they love,—to regard it as a kindly door, opening for their happy re-union with the loved (not lost), and to exclaim with hope and joy, "I can now trace the shining path that lies beyond the grave.

"Its rays now light my spirit up, and save
My soul from constant dread; dispels the fears
That hung a funeral pall o'er all my years;
Now can I greet the message which shall come,
To call me hence, as summons from my home;
Then with my ebbing breath triumphant say,
As the rapt spirit sighs itself away,—
Oh Death, thy sting is robbed of all its pain!
Oh Grave, thy victory to me is gain!"

As I said before, Spiritualism is the science or philosophy of the soul. It proves its existence, its indestructibility; it teaches us that though the body be dead the soul still lives and loves, and that it cares for and delights to communicate with those who still dwell in the physical body.

The rationalist, the materialist, having no religious prejudices to warp his mind which is ever open to receive evidence whithersoever its results may lead him, and recognizing the great axiomatic truth to which I have before referred, *viz.*, that all phenomena in nature or all effects are the result of causes operating for their production, and not the blind and wayward results of chance—is usually willing to examine philosophically the evidence which spiritualism affords of the soul's immortality.

I will now present the case of such an one, knowing how hopeless is the future to him, desiring that he should receive the same hopes and happiness of which I am possessed, and I ask him to investigate the subject which he has perhaps only heard mentioned with ridicule, especially if his information has been derived from our brethren in the Church. Now, as he starts upon his tour of investigation, his attention is first of all directed to the physical phenomena, as these are the alphabet or rudiments of our science or philosophy. I hold out to him the hope that he may yet be able to gather sufficient evidence to convince him that what he has regarded as death, is but the door to real life. He now sets himself to work to glean the evidence that can be furnished, and having accumulated the facts he weighs and sifts them thoroughly, applying the keenest powers of his reason in his endeavors to arrive at truth; and I venture to say that few will fail in finding satisfactory proof thereof, if they enter upon the investigation in a spirit of candor and with a simple desire to know what truth is. But how, it may be asked, is this information to be obtained? I answer, in the same manner as all other scientific truths. The facts or phenomena are to be gleaned through the medium of the five senses, as these are the only avenues of the mind for communication with the external world by man in his ordinary or normal condition; and the mind depending upon the integrity of the senses, and upon the truthfulness of the impressions which its receives through them, for it has no other mode of gaining a knowledge of facts, sits in judgment upon what it has thus accumulated and renders its verdict accordingly, making use of the senses and relying upon them, and gathering the facts coming through them, which he knows to be first step towards knowledge. He consequently places himself in communication with these sources of the physical phenomena which are the basis of our belief. These are obtained at times through the medium of all the senses, but principally through those of hearing and seeing. To obtain these we will now suppose he calls upon Mrs. Brown, one of the original Rochester mediums, (formerly Mrs. Fox). Here come raps upon the table, upon the furniture, the walls of the room, and upon his own person. Through them by means of the alphabet, names of deceased friends are spelled, and affectionate communications received. In vain he looks for magnetic or electrical apparatus, or the paraphanalia belonging to the juggler's art, and he goes away with his curiosity increased and himself mystified regarding the cause of the sounds; and that some cause exists he is well aware. He next visits Dr. Slade. Here he sits at the table, in the broad light of the day. The doctor takes a clean slate, places a bit of pencil upon it of the size of a grain of wheat; he rests his left hand upon the top of the table and with his right grasps the frame of the slate at one end. This is now thrust under the table next the top, with his hands in full view. Soon he hears rapid writing upon the slate, the letters dotted and crossed, and then a rap indicating that they are to remove it. Now, what does he discover? A communication in the hand-writing, and signed by the name of some departed friend, telling him "I still live." And this occurs when the medium is an entire stranger, and the friend not in his thoughts. The doctor now takes an accordeon by the bellows end in one hand, while the other rests upon the table under his own; immediately the instrument is extended, he sees the movement of the keys without mortal contact, and listens to the tune of "Home, Sweet Home," played with infinite sweetness.

Next he goes the Photographic artist Mumler, and although an entire stranger, yet when he sits for his picture, perhaps the loved face and form of some dear departed friend long since passed over the river, is developed upon the plate with him. Now he visits Mr. Foster of

New York, who says to him: "I see by your side a little girl with blue eyes and golden hair, with a scar across the left cheek and a limp in her gait, as though her right limb was lame." Again, Mr. Foster says: "I see an elderly lady looking affectionately towards you. Her hair is silvered and her complexion fair. She says she was thrown from a carriage and killed by a blow upon the head twelve years ago this month, and here you will find her name." And as he bares his arm you behold the name of Sarah Wilmot in crimson raised letters. Mr. Foster says, "Do you recognize these." Overwhelmed with astonishment he replies you have correctly described my mother and my daughter.

To test the matter still further, he now addresses a letter to some friend in spirit life, encloses and seals it in such a manner that it cannot be tampered with without detection, and places it in the hands of Mr. Mansfield. Soon his letter is returned unopened and answered as though by the friend addressed, and frequently giving names of other spirit friends, and referring to incidents known only to them and himself.

He now calls upon Mrs. Kegwin, and most wonderful physical phenomena are produced. Mrs. Kegwin is a plain, upright woman, living in the country, the wife of a farmer. Here he sees musical instruments played upon withouth visible contact, hands and faces shown claiming to be produced by spirit agency, and in such a manner that he knows it to be physically impossible for the medium to produce them through her own organs.

Again, he enters the lecture room where Mrs. Lizzie Kizer is engaged, and he is astonished and delighted with the flood of beautiful thoughts—with the profound truths springing from the lips of an uneducated and uncultivated woman. He sees her step forward at the close of the lecture and pass about among the many strangers in the audience, selecting one here and another there, telling them she sees their spirit friends standing near, particularizes, describing their persons and giving their names, and even the peculiar articles of dress they were accustomed to wear in earth-life, and have now in appearance assumed that they may be recognized and acknowledged by those whom she addresses.

Now he calls upon Mrs. Francis O. Hyzer, who, alike with the last, has had but few educational advantages, and in answer to a mental question asked of the poet Burns, if he still loves and is wedded to his Highland Mary, he receives the following response, which all who are familiar with the poet's style will recognize as his, and as being equal in spirit and power to his happiest effusions:

Fair Lady, that I come to you,
A stranger bard, fu weel I ken,
For ye've known naught of me save through
The lays I poured through Scotia's glen;
But when I speak o' gliding Ayr,
O' hawthorn shades, and fragrant ferns,
O' Doon, and highland Mary fair,
Mayhap ye'll think o' Robert Burns.

I am the lad, and why I'm here,
I heard the gude dame when she said,
She'd know in joyous spirit sphere
If Burns was wi' his Mary wed.
I sought to tell her o' our joy,
No muckle impress could I make,
And lady, I have flown to see
If ye'd my message to her take.

Tell her that when I passed from earth,
My angel lassie crowned wi' flowers,
Met me wi' glowing love-lit torch
And led me to the nuptial bowers;
That all we dreamed o' wedded bliss,
And more, was meeted to us there;
And sweeter was my dearie's kiss,
Than on the flowery banks o' Ayr.

Where love's celestial fountains played,
And rosebuds burst and seraphs sang,
And myrtle twined our couch to shade,
I clasped the love I'd mourned sa lang;
And while by angel harps were played
The bonny bridal serenade;
Though na gowned priest the kirk rite said,
Burns was wi Highland Mary wed.

There's na destroying death frosts here,
To nip the hope buds ere they bloom;
The bridal tour is through the spheres;
Eternity's the honeymoon.
And now, kind lady, if ye'll bear,
These words unto the anxious dame,
I think I can ye so reward,
Ye'll ne'er be sorry that I came.

If I know what inspiration means I here recognise evidence of spirit breathings.

Our friend now visits the medium Home, and through him he receives communications, professing to come from the departed with most staggering evidences of their origin and truth. His hand is grasped where he knows no mortal hand exists, and he sees the medium suspended in the air without material contact, susceptible to the senses. Having observed these things, he now makes himself familiar with the literature of spiritualism, and in this he finds that the evidendences of the spirits return from the land of the leal, occurring spontaneously, unasked and unsought for, by persons in all ages, and in all parts of the world are almost overwhelming, coming like a constant revelation from God to man.

Having satisfied himself of the occurrence of the phenomena, and of the impossibilty of his being imposed upon by the professed mediums, and feeling full confidence in the integrity of his senses, he now sits down with the facts he has accummulated to see whether they can be explained satisfactorily in any other manner than by spirit influence.

In the first place he takes up the purely physical phenomena of sound and the movement of ponderable articles. In these alone he says: I see no proof of spirit power; to be sure I could see no cause to produce them, but still I can easily conceive that such results may be produced by some force in nature analagous to electricity, but with which we are perhaps at present unacquainted. And were this all the evidence he possessed his conclusions might be considered rational and legitimate.

But hold, he says. Before I decide this positively, I must go a step further. What means this writing which I have so frequently received with the names of departed friends, relating incidents which transpired during their earth life? Here is something more than electricity—something more than the operation of one of the forces in nature—and what is it? Why, this is intelligence! I know he says that sounds may be produced by electricity, for the thunder following the lightning's flash tells me that; and I know that physical bodies can be moved by the same cause, for I have seen it shiver the giant oak and hurl it to the dust. But electricity cannot think; it is a powerful force in nature, but blind and aimless. Sounds and the movements of ponderable bodies may result from physical causes, but thought can only be exhibited where there is an intelligent will power. Galvanism, magnetism, electricity, and odic force he says are powerful elements in nature, but they cannot reason, reflect, compare, will, or exercise memory. This is the province of mind. He first becomes convinced of the truth of the occurrence of the physical phenomena, and connected with and producing them, he discovers thought, intelligence, mind; and this mind he knows has no material surroundings ordinarily visible to mortal eye in its normal condition, and this he calls spirit, and that the spirit is what it claims to be,—a disembodied intelligence, once occupying a body like his own, he believes, from the irresistible evidence of its identity which the spirit offers. A stranger presents himself at a bank with a draft payable to John Brown, which is himself. Now the officers ot the bank have never seen John Brown, but they have his signature. They ask the stranger to write his name. This they find to be a fac simile of the known signature of John Brown which they have in their possession, and they pay the draft without hesitation. We recognise the right of spirit to identify itself in the same manner.

A Mason applies at the door of a Lodge for admission. If he is able to give the signs and responses correctly he is admitted, as by these he is identified and known to be what he claims. And when spirit presents itself and imparts information which is known only to that spirit, we can by no rule of logic attribute the intelligence thus communicating, to any other source than that from which it claims to come.

Our materialist friend is satisfied now of the truth of that which he never before believed, *viz.*, that mind,—spirit,—can and does exist outside and independent of the physical body, and to his infinite joy he has received satisfactory proof that they can and do return, endeavoring to exercise a watchful care over earthly friends, and often bringing messages of love to cheer them in their life journey, showing that their affection outlives the change called death, and often attracts them to those they love. But our christian friends have another answer to all this bosh, as one of their priests in my hearing a short time since, in his ignorance and with malicious hate was pleased to term it. They have got an old devil who can accomplish almost any thing he chooses, and when all other arguments fail, they bring him up as a kind of *corps de reserve* to battle for them. This old devil explains the whole mystery, and since some of them, without seeking it, have been witnesses of these phenomena, and are constrained to admit the intelligence connected therewith being proof of mind, they have undertaken to lay the whole thing upon his shoulders.

Said an eminent clergyman in one of our orthodox churches, and a professor in one of our Colleges, to me recently: "I have thoroughly investigated this matter, and am satisfied that the occurences do take place as represented. Now," said he, "there are but two ways of accounting for them—one by physical, and the other by spiritual agencies. I know, said he, that it is not the former, for I have not only seen ponderable bodies moved without physical contact, but I have seen intelligence displayed that no mere force in nature could produce. Consequently, the only conclusion I can come to is, that the causes are spiritual. But, said he, I have warned my Church to have nothing to do with it, for I am satisfied that the devil is at the bottom of it all. And the principal reason he advanced in favor of its diabolical origin was, that what they taught did not agree with the teachings of the church. But before he left me I found the good parson had more faith in angelic ministrations than he had before admitted, when he told me that he believed that the spirits of his daughter and mother were about him, and that he often felt their influence, and received impressions from them, and that the thoughts of it often gave him great pleasure.

But, our christian friends should remember that they are handling a two-edged sword, and that the same blow they aim at the destruction of modern spiritualism will sever every thread of evidence which the bible furnishes them of spirit communion. Now, we will take their own rule by which to be judged. Jesus Christ says: "By their own works ye shall know them." And again, "Believe not all the, spirits but try them, and see whether they be of God." Now I submit the question to you my friends, which, by this rule has the best claim to a devilish origin,—that command which the priests of old, mentioned in the Bible say they received from the Lord, to go out and make war upon a neighboring nation, bidding them slay the old men and the old women and the infants, to disembowel with their swords those who were expecting to become mothers, and to distribute the captive young maidens among the priests to be their mistresses, (a command so horrible that their fabled devil and hell could invent nothing more brutal,) or the doctrines taught by modern spiritualism, to cultivate the higher elements of humanity, to deal justly and love truth, to succor the weak, and deal gently with the erring; to minister to the suffering, and seek in every way to elevate mankind and advance them in the scale of intellectual, moral and social progress. If the former be of God, we disclaim all allegiance to such, and say it is not the one we worship; and if the latter be the teachings of the prince of darkness, then, say I, blessed be the devil, for no matter what name you give him, we prefer to accept the teachings of that spirit of truth and goodness which tells us to do that which our consciences know to be right and admonishes us against error and wrong; but we expect to receive from the religious bigots of our fashionable churches the same denunciations that were heaped upon the founder of the christian faith by the Jews of old, who were the respectable and orthodox religionists of their day, when they said, *He hath a devil.*

Spiritualists believe that when the spirit quits the body, its intellectual and moral status is in no wise changed by the transfer. They belive that when evil, gross, and malignant natures drop their earthly covering they awake in their new life with the same propensities, and that there as here, they bring their punishment as a natural effect or consequence of their own acts, and that those who in this life have endeavored to live in harmony with the laws which Deity has instituted, and have thereby added much to their happiness here, will find themselves in their new life possessed of the same ennobling aspirations after truth and all that is elevated, and which will continue to yield the same happiness in the future as in their present condition of existence; but they also believe that all may, and ultimately will advance to a higher state of knowledge and happiness as they are taught by their experience, and understand and appreciate divine and infinite truth. They believe that men's natures are in no wise changed by death, and that a deceitful nature here will prove a deceitful spirit still, should it come and communicate with us from the realms of the departed, but that the truthful and good will retain the same character there as in earth life.

The inspiration or breathing of thought from spirits to mortals is not new to man. It has come both from good and bad spirits in all ages of the world. We read in the Bible that the Lord sent lying spirits, who spake through the mouths of the prophets of old, in order to deceive the people, and we are taught to use our judgment to determine what is true and what is false, even as the bank officer assures himself that the representations of the payee of the draft are truthful. We use our judgment thus in the everyday affairs of life, and we should but stultify ourselves did we not exercise the same caution in spiritual matters.

From the other shore, the voices of those who have passed over the flood come back to tell us that the doctrine of a hell of fire and brimstone is a fable cunningly devised to excite men's fears, but that every man is happy there, as here, in proportion as he cultivates the God-like elements of his nature, and that the orthodox devil is a myth, but that evil as well as good exists in the heart of every man.

> "The soul should no longer with terror behold,
> The red waves of wrath with which priests would engulph her,
> For science ignores the rxistence of hell,
> And chemistry finds better uses for sulphur."

Spiritualism is not new, but its correct in'erpretation has been rendered only of late years; and it has come as a source of joy and hope to every one who reasons, thinks and endeavors to learn and understand the truth, and desires to be delivered from the yoke of priestly intolerance—not that the rack and fagot are still to be feared, for, thank God, the intelligence of the age has as we hope banished them from the earth forever; but those claiming spiritual authority even now, to the limits of their power, exercise the same devilish hate which actuated them of old, and with a malignity worthy of their mythical arch fiend, launch forth their anathemas, and attempt to place the ban of their curse upon us and use their influence, socially, to ostracise those who honestly differ from them in belief, especially the believers in modern spiritualism. Perhaps this may be considered harsh language, but I know whereof I speak.

It is not many months since a clergyman in one of our so-called evangelical churches of this city, stood up in his Church and villified the spiritualists, and also counselled his flock not to patronize them in business, but to ignore them socially and starve them out of town. This same priest, while addressing the Young Men's Christian Association, of which he was a member, while summing up in his self-righteous style the wickedness with which they the pure and spotless lambs of this world had to contend, held up the believers in spiritualism as objects of ridicule and contempt, and with his wicked and malicious tongue outraged and misrepresented them to a degree that would have made his own devil blush for shame, on acconnt of the slanderous lies he uttered. After enumerating the various vices of the day—rum drinking, gambling, and every form of immorality, he concluded his tissue of falsehood and abuse by saying: "But worse than all these are the spiritualists." If, instead of this, he had said he feared them more than all other forms of opposition to priestly tyranny, he would undoubtedly have been correct; and you may feel assured that where there is so much smoke and clamor; that the fire of spiritualism has penetrated their strongholds, and with God's blessing we hope soon to beat down their opposition to truth, and put them and their errors to rout. This was from one of the lambs who professes to teach the doctrines inculcated by the meek, charitable, and loving Jesus. Beautiful lambs of

Christ's flock are these. God save us from their tender mercies; but their voice betrays them and shows that beneath the external emblems of innocence and purity they but hide the fangs of the wolf. But I find that if the spiritualist, whom they so hate, has aught in the way of patronage to bestow, they are perfectly willing to receive it, probably acting upon the same principle as did the Israelites when they fled from Egypt, when every man and woman, by Divine command as they declared, borrowed gold and silver, jewels and raiment from the Egyptians, that they might spoil them.

And I can point you to a so-called divine in this city who recently delivered a tirade in his church against the spiritualists, and was so anxious to have it appear in print that he might in a more pnblic manner traduce us, that he hurried from his church to the printing office on Sunday evening, and read proof for two hours while the poor printers were at work setting type for him, although but two weeks before he delivered a discourse on the sanctity and for the better observance of the Christian Sabbath; and although his old arch devil did not inform against him, perhaps because he considered him a faithful servant; yet his inconsistency was so glaring, that with infinite disgust, the printer's devil did. Is it possible that such men can have the audacity to stand up and call themselves God's ministers. If so, their acts sadly belie their professions. And for the benefit of such I would repeat the language of Alexander McLachlam.

"Who are the priests whom God appoints;
Whose heads with wisdom He annoints,
To spread His truth abroad;
Not those who mumble o'er the creeds,
But those who plant truth's living seeds
Are the true priests of God.

"Humanity, what hast thou gained,
From those the churches have ordained;
They've but increased thy load;
Apologists in every clime,
Of outrage, tyranny and crime—
They're not the priests of God.

"Ah! 'tis to the uncanonized,
The persecuted and despised,
Tnat God reveals the light;
And they're the fearless ones that rise
Against earth's consecrated lies,
And battle for the right.

"They are the poets, bards and seers,
Whose words draw sympathetic tears
E'en from the stubborn clod,
And bear us on the wings of song
Above defilement, blight and wrong,
They are the priests of God.

"The heralds of a hope sublime,
Forerunners of a better time,
The leaders of the van;
And fearlessly they're marching forth,
Proclaiming over all the earth
The brotherhood of man.

"They wear no sacerdotal weeds,
They know no churches, sects nor creeds,
But in the truth are strong;
They're the priests whom God ordains
To break men's spiritual chains,
And overthrows the wrong.

"Yes, they're the priests of the most high,
Whose temples are the earth and sky,
The sea and running brook;
Interpreters of nature's lines,
And of the symbols and the signs
In her eternal book.

"They read God's scriptures everywhere,
In stellar worlds, in sea, in air,
And in the flowery sod;
They only are the true divines
Through whom the light of nature shines—
The great high priests of God.

"Communion with the Saints above,
Relying on Almighty love,
The universal plan,
They feel their own divinity,
And find the glorious trinity
In nature, God, and man.

"Mediums or bards, what e'er ye are,
Who bring us tidings from afar,
To brighten our abode,—
Through whom the heavens communicate
The glories of the future state,
Ye're the high priests of God."

Said a member of one our orthodox churches to me recently, when speaking upon the subject of spiritualism: "I don't want anything to do with it. I do not considerable it respectable. Why, just look at the people who attend those meetings; they're not the fashionable people, and those who lead in society, but are made up mostly of the common laboring class." Good God! and has it come to this? Has all the blood that has been shed in the name of religion from the earliest promulgation of christianity until now, and which, through the instigation of religious fanaticism, has dyed the earth in human gore, has this all been shed simply to build up a church to minister to human pride, and for the display of fine apparel? Has it come to this, that the so-called religions of the day are nothing but a mockery set apart for the use of the rich, and if any benefits are received from them by the poor, they must be gathered like the crumbs by Lazarus from under the rich man's table? Alas! the history of the church and the evidences we see before us, prove it to be too true. Under the pretense of pleasing God, but in reality to minister to their own pride and vanity, they build structures for his pretended worship, so costly, that if the salvation of the poor depended upon listening to the instruction imparted therein, they might as well make uo their minds at once to be damned; for but few families dependent upon their daily labor for their bread could afford to eat the so-called bread of life dispensed in these costly and elegant institutions. And were the poor and despised Nazarine, the founder of their religion, and the humble fishermen of Galilee to again appear and say as they did old, "Sell all thou hast and give it to the poor. Look not out for to-morrow. It is easier for a camel to go through a needle's eye than for a rich man to enter the kingdom of heaven," inculcating charity, universal benevolence, poverty and dependence upon God for daily bread, they would regard them as madmen and drive them from their synagogues.

And thus has it ever been in all ages of the world, when a religion becomes mossy with age,—when priestly dogmas have been substituted for spiritual truths, priding themselves upon their antiquity and consequent respectability—they offer scorn in place of reason, and when God's children ask for bread they give them a stone.

But, says our orthodox churchman, who, being rich, therefore feels that he is respectable, Jesus Christ certainly did not mean that. He did not mean what he said when he commanded us to sell all we had and give it to the poor. Oh, no! Well, my christian friend, perhaps you know what Jesus Christ meant, a great deal better than he did himself. And if he did not mean to teach a life of poverty and self-denial to his followers, why did he say so? and why did he not use language to express what he did mean?

All new ideas and the promulgation of all great truths, both now and ever, has met with opposition and persecution from the conservative portion of the world, and while old ideas and opinions are considered respectable, the leaders in the van of progress have always been objects of the bigot's hate and scorn. But, thank God, we have still been able to live and enjoy the luxury of thinking independently, and following the dictates of our own consciences and convictions of right, and recognizing no Master but the Great Supreme.

But I turn from this picture with its dark and damning shades—a subject it seemed fit I should review, but with feelings more of sorrow than anger—to the brighter one which now presents itself to us as we behold the progress of our glorious philosophy. Not that spiritualists are zealots in the work of proselyting the world and bringing all to their faith; for they believe that all men will sooner or later, as time and death bear them on, of necessity admit the truth of what they teach, but knowing the happiness which their belief imparts, they would be glad to have all share its consolations and partake of its joys. Still our philosophy teaches us the right of every man to free and independent thought, and learns us to respect the honest differences of another's opinions equally with those which coincide with our own. Freedom, mental freedom is the word, and we recognize this as the most sacred and inalienable right of man. And as the world grows older we believe that more liberal and enlightened views will prevail, and that men will in time learn that truth is not elicited by attempting to shut out the light and choking down investigation, but by the free and full discussion of all those points where doubt and honest difference of opinion exists, not by erecting credal walls in which to imprison the minds of men and prevent them from looking over into the great ocean of recognized as well as undiscovered truth which lies beyond, bnt by offering every facility to the mind in its search for ultimate and supreme knowledge. And we hail with pleasure the return of this day which signalizes the recognition of the advent of modern spiritualism, a day which in the coming ages will be hailed with joy by unborn millions. And as years and physical change creeps over us while floating down life's river, may the soul still retain its freshness and youth, growing brighter as the experience of life enables us to correct the errors of the past, and gathering rich harvests of wisdom as we are enabled to solve the profound mysteries and problems of existence. And as our barks are headed for the evergreen shores, and we musingly reflect on the past while gathering bright hopes for the future, may our hearts be filled with unspeakable joy as earth fades from view, and with exultant delight break forth in rapturous song—

"And I sit and think as the sunset's gold
  Is flushing river and hill and shore,
I shall one day stand by the waters cold,
  And list for the sound of the boatman's oar.
I shall watch the gleam of the flapping sail,
  I shall hear the boat as it gains the strand,
I shall pass from sight with the boatman pale,
  To the better shore of the spirit land;
I shall know the loved who have gone before,
  And joyfully sweet will the meeting be,
When over the river, the peaceful river,
  The angel of death shall carry me."

ALSO, A

SUBSEQUENT ADDRESS,

DELIVERED AT THE SAME PLACE, ON THE QUESTION OF

WHAT BENEFIT IS

SPIRITUALISM TO MAN?

WHAT BENEFIT IS SPIRITUALISM TO MAN?

It has always been the course adopted by conservatism, revolving in its beaten track, and ever returning to the point from whence it started, when overwhelmed in its opposition, by the discovery and recognition of truth by the world, to discourage all efforts at progress by the *cui bono*, or what benefit, which is always asked whenever their Rip Van Winkle sleep is disturbed by one ray of light peering in upon their darkened souls, or any new idea which is subversive of their time-honored opinions and customs is gleaned from the great realm of truth. To them all reformers and progressionists are madmen, innovators upon their ancient customs, and disturbers of the harmony which has existed so long, that they regard naught which opposes it as respectable. Their course in this respect is not a novel one. It is but a repetition of the world's history as we read it in every age. But were it not for these reformers and progressionists, the world might still be in the same condition of barbarism and ignorance which existed during the childhood of our race. They are the winds and storms of the intellectual and moral world, which while they may for a season disturb the order and quiet which are simply the result of mental inertia, yet they bear in their blast the elements of life and health, and stir up and purify the foul, stagnant and narcotizing atmosphere of conservatism, whose tendency has ever been to starve the mind and fetter the soul.

All newly recognized truths, whether in science or religion, have ever been met by this class in the same spirit, and the oft-reiterated question of what is its use, is thrust upon him who leads in the van of progress, who teaches any new social, scientific or religious idea, who inaugurates any reform in the moral world, or attempts to correct any social wrong. It is thrust upon the man of science as he seeks to unlock the mysteries of nature, and wrench by power of mind the secrets from her bosom. It meets the astronomer when with telescopic vision he sweeps the heavens and brings from their mysterious and remotest depths the infinitude of worlds which appear like continents of starry dust floating in the immensity of space. It follows the philosopher as he unfolds the mysteries of nature, and seems almost to rend the veil which hides the infinite, and solves those problems which had ever been regarded as too deep to fathom except by the mind of omniscience. It is the drag rope which binds us to the past, and antogonizes the discoverer as he would direct his bark over the great ocean of truth which lies beyond him.

Every discovery in any department of knowledge—every perception of a previously unrecognized law—every fact which has for the first time been presennted to the world, extending our knowledge of the universe of matter or mind—in short, every discovery, fact, truth, or item of knowledge which is unfolded to the world, is a positive good; and he who adds one iota to the sum of human knowledge may be regarded as a benefactor to his race. And as the laws which govern spirit life and the modes of its return and manifesting itself to those yet lingering in the earth sphere are recognized and understood—as the two worlds are brought nearer together, and the scenes of earth and spirit life almost mingle into one—as man loses more of the grossness of the outer phase of existence, and the inner or spiritual sense or vision is unfolded, and he perceives the soul of things, or the spiritual, which underlies the material,—and as with vision of the seer he looks through the clouds of earth and sense, and is brought *en rapport* with the inner life, and comprehends its relation to the outer phase of existence, then shall he more fully recognize and understand the wondrous laws which govern his being, and learn why the soul is ever yearning and grasping for hidden truth which many solve the mysteries of life; for he will then discover that it is its intuitive longing to return the source from whence it sprang, the infinite source of life and of light, and thus to assimilate itself to the great fountain of its being, Yet we still continue to hear from religious conservatism its deprecating cry of, what use is spiritualism to man, and what good is it doing in the world; and I trust I may be able to answer the question in a manner satisfactory to those who ask it in sincerity, and are ignorant of the facts and reasons which have brought conviction of its truth with its gratifying results to our minds. But it is not in this spirit of candid enquiry that the question is usually asked by the christian clergy, who have ever been foremost in misrepresenting our opinions and maligning us. They probably excuse themselves for their misrepresentations, and satisfy their consciences for the utterance of falsehood, on the ground that a fiction is excusable if uttered in the name of religion; and consider the reasons as valid which the religious fanatics of former days gave for their conduct, *viz.*, that the end justifies the means. Men may wilfully state that which they know to be false or make representations to the injury of another, which they know to be untrue, being instigated by their prejudices, and may seek to excuse themselves under such pretexts; but I know of no other name which will properly apply to such statements but lies:

"There are popular lies and political lies,
And lies that stick fast between buying and selling;
And lies of politeness, convential lies,
(Which scarcely are reckoned as such in the telling;)
There are lies of sheer malice, and slanderous lies,
From those who delight to peck filth like a pigeon,
But the oldest, and far most respectable lies,
Are those that are told in the name of religion."

They are instigated, no doubt, by that spirit of intolerance and opposition to free thought which has ever characterized them as a body, decrying reason, and substituting that which they have decided to be inspiration, altogether in its stead, and for which they claim infallibility. It is not so much that which is intrinsically evil which they oppsse, as that which is antagonistic to their dogmas, and spiritual supremacy. They will take a professed atheist by the hand, and admit the infidel and disbeliever in the immortality of the soul to full social fellowship, because they have no fear of their influence, well knowing that they have nothing to offer men in the place of the hopes they would destroy; but when the materialist through the evidence we offer men is enabled to believe in the soul as an entity, which is indestructible by physical death, and declares to the world that the evidence he has received from us has convinced him of the truth of our philosophy, then are the batteries of their slander turned upon him and the cause he has embraced.

In adopting this course they are but carrying out the spirit of their own, and all other religions, whether Christian, Jewish, Mahomedan or Pagan, which claim to have an infallible rule of right in what they regard as God's word received through inspiration, and which they contend can therefore contain no error; and this has been the authority in all ages for religious fanatics to commit some of the most devilish atrocities that the world has ever witnessed. They are right, and all who differ from them are in the wrong, and it is only for want of power that they do not use force to compel men to their ways of thinking when they cannot persuade them.

This is the same self-righteous, dogmatic, arrogant, and persecuting spirit, which gave the inquisition its victims, has ever sought to enslave the minds of men, and suppress free thought; setting up their own opinions, and endeavoring to compel obedience to them, no matter how stultifying to the intelligence or the enlightened moral sense; attempting to stop the wheels of progress, and bound the field of religious enquiry by the narrow limits of their own creeds, and to shut out the light and knowledge which the soul might receive in its yearnings and search after truth. And in confirmation of what I utter I have but to refer to the combined and energetic effort which is now being made to overturn that guarantee of religious freedom, and free thought, the constitution of our country, and incorporating with it those provisions which shall make their religion compulsory and free thought obnoxious. This is the spirit of the old theology which is rapidly becoming a thing of the past, which had its origin in an age of barbarism and ignorance, and which if it ever was adapted to the childhood of our race, when force was substitued for reason, and religious terrors held over the mind to compel obedience to sanitary measures and police regulations, cannot be so regarded in the nineteenth century when the light shed by science and reason, and the growth of mind has given us the right and authority to assert our claims, to have our manhood recognized, and to enjoy untrammelled the privilege of using the intellect which God has given us for the purpose he intended.

The day has passed in which the minds of men can be thus bound, or in which they can hope to arrest the onward and ever onward march of untrammelled and progressive thought. And although in their frenzied fury they may hurl themselves against the great wave of spiritual truth which is now sweeping over the earth; yet they cannot impede its progress, which, irresistible as an avalanche, will overwhelm all who oppose it. The time is rapidly passing when men will be content to feed on the husks of an effete and impracticable religion; when wisdom and truth, the angels of progress, are scattering the bread of life on every hand; when men will submit at the dictum of a bigoted priesthood to smother the reason which God has given them, to determine between truth and error or between right and wrong,—neither are they to be frightened by the bugbear of an omnipotent devil whenever they attempt to look over the theological wall which their ghostly advisers have built up around them. I have thus referred to this subject to show that the so-called religion of the day, which originated in a past age, and over which decay is now creeping, is a system which fosters mental bondage, and is antagonistic to progress. Its teachers ignoring reason as a guide, and substituting what they regard as the infallible records of inspiration in its stead, and attempting to convince us of its supremacy by reasoning with us to prove that reason itself is utterly unreliable; in which case, and if its decisions are not trustworthy and not a reliable guide, then they but stultify themselves in every argument they use; and if not reliable, then why do they receive as authority the decisions of those councils which met to determine upon the reliability and authority of what the church has received as its sacred canons; and if in that case it was to be trusted, have we not equally with them a right to use our reason to determine whether *their* decisions were correct or not.

Reason, we believe, to be the final arbiter, and its voice must decide for each and every one all mooted questions. This is its province and its right, and is recognized as such by all mental philosophers worthy of the name, although the term rationalist is usually applied as a name of reproach by religious bigots to all who claim for reason and experience superlative authority. But while the popular religions of the day but fetter the mind, the philosophy whose doctrines we have embraced, and advocate, have a different mission, which is to free the world from mental slavery, and the motto borne aloft in blazing letters upon our banner is *Freedom, mental Freedom, to the whole race of man.*

The spiritualist ever appeals to the reason, and while he shows the errors of false religious systems, he demonstrates to man the certainty of a life in the future of intellectual activity and happiness, which the christian religion but faintly shadows, and the jewish sacred writings scarce anywhere acknowledge. And I am satisfied from statements that have often been made to me by members of christian churches, that with many, owing to the dimness of the spiritual light which the church has to offer, that their faith in the soul's immortality is so feeble, that to them death truly comes as a king of terrors, and they look forward with fear and trembling to what they call and seem to regard as the summons of the dread messenger, lest the soul spark be extinguished by death in the eternal gloom of annihilation.

It is but a short time since an intelligent and respected member of one of our christian churches said to me: "I do not wonder that you spiritualists are not afraid to die; and if I believed as you do, I should not have any dread of it myself, for you appear to feel as though you had positive knowledge of the future; but with us it is hope, which we call belief, but which we know but very little about." This remark indicated to my mind a most forlorn hope, but not that certainty in belief which the evidence we have received gives us. I replied that spiritualists equally with others dreaded the sundering of earthly ties and associations, and separation from the pleasant scenes of this life, and from the objects we have known and loved; and equally with them instinctively recoil from the prospect of physical dissolution; and that we also believe that the soul can better advance its interests by accumulating the knowledge and experience which may be gained by living out the full term of matured earthly life allotted to man; but that the future gave us no fear and that the evidence we had received had given us a knowledge of a future life, and an assurance of meeting and recognizing the loved ones who had preceeded us.

Said a prominent member, and one regarded as a main pillar in one of our orthodox churches to me not long since: I believe that when man dies he sleeps in the grave and has no conscious existence until the general resurrection which we are told will take place at the end of the world; but christians believing that Christ rose from the dead, rely on his promise that he will raise and reanimite them at that time. But, said he again, and in a voice of painful sadness, I have very grave doubts whether that ever takes place. Poor man! From my heart I pitied him, for I knew that he had tried to be a consistent member of the church for many years, and still endeavored to wrap himself in her garments, which with his mental growth had become to short to cover him, hoping against hope, and still clinging to the faint and feeble evidence the church had to offer of the soul's immortality, and oft asking himself the same question which was said to have been propounded by Job in his dreary unbelief, if a man die shall he live again? and the answer he was as often compelled to render, as he endeavored to solve the great problem of future existence, was as hopeless as the conclusion arrived at by him whom the bible declared to have been the wisest of men, *viz.:* That there was no reward in the grave whither he was going; that death was a sleep which knew no waking, and that there was nothing better for a man than that he should enjoy the present hour, for no man could tell what should be after him. And as with a heart shorouded in gloom, he found himself approaching the period of life when he knew the silver cord must soon be loosed, he acknowledged that the future was to him but a cheerless waste, and all his hopes of a happy life beyond the grave almost extinguished. I do not believe that all who pin their faith in a future life on the bible, are thus hopeless, but I do know that many, very many in our churches are as despondent as himself, and that many others would be glad to obtain evidence which should confirm their feeble hopes.

Said a loving mother to me, who had long been a member of a christian church, and who had just lost a darling child,—I wish you would tell me what you know about our friends who are dead returning to us, for I hear that you believe that they do so; and as she told me the story of her great and crushing grief, and the fountain of her bitter tears were unlocked and welled up from the depths of her breaking heart, while her frame was convulsed with agony. She cried out in her desolation, Oh, if I knew that my darling lived and loved me still, I could bear it; but beyond the grave all is so dark, and we know so little what comes after death. My minister has been here, prayed for, and tried to console me. He has told me that which I have so often heard before, that Christ had passed through death, and knew what suffering was, and felt for and sympathized with us. But, said she, this does not satisfy me; it does not lighten my anguish at all. What I want to know is, that my baby is alive and happy, and that it will again know me. If you can give me convincing assurances of this, I can bear my loss and you will save my heart from breaking.

Think you, my friends, that spiritualism has no consolations to offer to a heart like this that was breaking? Now, what was wanting to soothe this mother's sorrow? Not the stereotyped cant which her minister offered her as she had heard him offer to others frequently before, and which fell like lead upon her soul; but she wanted that which neither he nor her religion could give, undoubting assurances that her baby was alive and happy, and that she would be re-united with it. And as the proofs and assurances for which she longed, and which it is the mission of spiritualism to give, were received and treasured in her soul, her tears of anguish were turned to gems of joy, while despair fled, and the angel hope nestled in her bosom, as she sung,

"Now, when my weary aching eyes
With tears of anguish fill,
I brush them away, for I somehow feel,
That my darling is with me still."

Many years since I met a patriarchal looking man whose silvered head warned him that he was fast approaching the period when he would test for himself the realities of the unknown future. In conversation I found him to be a gentleman of much intelligence and culture. He told me that, knowing I was a spiritualist, he had come to talk with me upon the subject. He said he had been a member of an orthodox church for over forty years, that the friends with whom he travelled the road of life had one after another dropped by his side, until nearly all had passed over the flood. And now, said he, as I approach the river myself, on whose banks my age and infirmities warn me I shall soon stand, I have been looking about me and trying to make the necessary preparations for the journey. I have been carefully weighing the evidence on which I had relied, and as a result I find my mind filled with most distressing doubts of the immortality of the soul; I find my belief of it to be purely a matter of religious faith and hope, and not founded on that evidence which gives positive assurance, such as I desire to have; that physical death is but the commencement of a higher life, and the bursting of soul from the web of mortality into a brighter, clearer, more expanded, and intellectual existence, where the infirmities of our grosser materiality neither fetter the mind nor corrupt the heart; and any satisfactory evidence I may receive of the spirit's return and manifesting itself, would of course be proof that they still live. While, said he, I had the prospect of many years before me, I was satisfied with what the church taught; but now as I stand upon the borders of life, I have to deal with realities; and I find the supposed proofs on which I had rested, crumbling beneath my feet; but if I can receive evidence confirmatory of my feeble hopes, which will demonstrate to me that life ends not here, then shall I emerge from the cloud which has so long rested over me, and the sunset of my life be golden and bright. All this was uttered in a voice and manner which showed but too clearly the hopelessness and despondency which reigned in the old man's bosom. And as I recounted my own experience and detailed the evidence on which we based the claims of our philosophy, the old man's eye grew bright and his voice quivered with emotion as he gathered like richest gems the facts I presented, and laid away among his heart's choicest treasures the reasons I advanced, and I felt that the bright angel hope had again spread her wings over him as he exclaimed: Oh! if this indeed be true, then shall I meet again with the dear friends who have passed on and left me alone and desolate in life.

Tell me not that spiritualism brings no happiness to man, and ask me no more what benefit it is to the world when the hearts of thousands who are just entering upon life's bright morning are made happy by its promises, and the hopes that it inspires, who are fortified by its consolations and enabled to meet life's reverses and vicissitudes with cheerfulness, and to look with comparative calmness upon the harvest of death as their friends fall beneath the mowers' scythe,—knowing as they do that the separation from the idols of their hearts is but for a moment. Tell me not it is a curse to the world when the old man, as he finds years with their accompanying infirmities relentlessly sapping his physical powers and bearing him in their remorseless grasp onward to the great ocean of eternity; as the ties which bind him to earthly life, one after another, become sundered; as he finds the soul's material envelope which in early years like a goodly bark bore him proudly and joyously along life's river, but which, having now almost reached her haven, lies battered and storm worn, and is fast grinding herself to fragments upon the rocks which line eternity's shore, while the seething waves of death are yawning to engulph her. Tell me not it is an old wive's tale, when from the midst of all this physical decay and ruin the soul is borne up and sustained by its firm conviction of the truth which the evidence of our philosophy has afforded him of the soul's immortality and destiny; and as he looks across the flood and fixes his eye upon the becon light of hope, and knowledge of a life to come which has been assured to him, he feels, that even now, before he has reached the shores of the immortals, he already in anticipation tastes their joys, as his soul is illuminated by the light beyond which pierces the veil of his earthly gloom, while the angel messengers from the evergreen shores, like Noah's dove, bear him the green leaves of promise from the bright land of the blest.

Tell me not that spiritualism is an evil to be shunned because it combats the teachings which the church still inculcates, which originated in the past, and should be buried with the barbarism of the age which gave them birth; because it protests against the diabolism, (mis-called religion,) which tortures innocent childhood and uncorrupted youth, with fears by day and terrific visions by night, of a surging fiery lake of molten sulphur into which they are liable at any moment to be hurled by him whom they call God, but whom they have invested with the attributes of a dragon, whose hellish maw is gaping to receive its childish victims and ghoul-like revelling in the feast of eternal death, and giving the tortured innocents no hope of escape from their fiery torments during the weary ages of eternity, while demons damned from every quarter haste to fill with fiercer anguish and despair their cup of horrors.

Are those fitting instructors of babes who, under the guise of acting as spiritual guides, would cloud the tender years of childhood which should be bright and happy, by teachings so dark and damnable that the savage inflicting his infernal tortures upon his victims might be regarded as an angel of love and mercy when compared with those teachers of childhood, whose chief delight would seem to be to add new fuel to the hell of horrors which they prepare for the torture of innocence.

On the other hand, the little child under the teachings of our philosophy, learns to look upon death and the future without fear. He is taught that the friends he has loved and whose bodies he has seen laid away in the earth, are with him still, watching over, loving, and caring for him. He sees the butterfly burst from the chrysalis, mount upward, and onward float, in its new world of sunlight and joy, and he is taught by this image that the soul is the man, and that the body is but a temporary earthly covering; that life is the school where the soul is taught by experience, and elevated and refined by suffering and adversity, till death bids it drop the worn body, which the freed spirit now casts off like a worn out garment, forever, as with the glad bound of one disenthralled it mounts upward from its earthly prison, no longer a worn but a happy and joyous being, freed from the infirmities of the body, and its intellectual capacity and activity increased, forever advancing in knowledge and goodness, and ever learning new lessons of wisdom as he roams through the universe of God: He is taught that in studying nature he is learning of the great soul of life and intelligence which energizes and animates the universe, and that this is the only infallible book and unalterable record which infinite wisdom has left to man, whose teachings are never contradictory, and never change, not giving a doctrine of love to the christian, and hate and revenge to the Jew, but yielding the same lessons of truth and wisdom to all people and in all ages, when properly interpreted. Think you not the child leads a more happy life with such a belief and such principles instilled as he is taught to behold divinity in the sunshine and the flowers, in the mountain torrent and the gurgling brook, to hear the voice of divine wisdom in the song of birds, and the soft and perfumed breezes of summer as, well as in the grand and majestic peais which follow in the wake of heaven's fires;—and that in studying the laws of nature he is making himself familiar with the attributes of God, and is learning more and more of the infinite soul of life which animates the whole material universe when he communes with nature, and learns her wondrous laws, and that to be a student of nature and obedient to her teachings is to be a child of God.

Our philosophy teaches men this great lesson, that happiness, for which all men seek, is to be obtained only by living in conformity with and obeying those laws which reasons and experience teach us the existence of, and which were instituted for the good of all. And is the direct reward and legitimate result of such a life; that we can know of the existence of law only by observing the unchangeableness of nature's operation,—by the resulting effects, and by the penalities which are inflicted when her ordinances are violated, yielding happiness when we live in conformity with them, even as pain, disorder, physical destruction and moral degradation follow their infraction. It teaches that the penalty for violated law is never remitted, and that the soul once tarnished by wrong can never be as bright and happy as though its lustre had never been dimmed by evil, which the conscience recognizes, and like a relentless judge condemns.

It teaches that love is the cord which not only binds human hearts together, but draws the soul with swift and willing feet from the paths of error and wrong to the ways of goodness, purity, and truth; that all attempts to terrify the soul into an appreciation and observance of moral obligations, by threats of torture and an exhibition of hate and vindictiveness, can have but one of the two effects, either to stir it up to fierce resistance, and to bid defiance to all attempts at coercion, or to crush and make it crouch in abject submission, which fear may induce, but never makes the heart better.

It is but recently that I was reading the remarks made by an orthodox clergyman, when speaking upon the subject of spiritualism, in which he stated that he considered its effects very bad, because it robbed men of a wholesome fear of death. Well! Perhaps he and I might differ in regard to what he considered wholesome. I recollect that all my early years were spent in the enjoyment of these same benefits or wholesome fears of death, as he regarded it, scarce daring to close my childish eyes in sleep lest death and the terrible hell might overtake me ere I awoke, and how, after having said my infant prayer to the good God above me, and the kind angel sleep had spread her wings over and at last soothed me to rest, I would start in my childish terror as fearful visions of damned and torturing fiends raved round me and filled the goblin haunted pit I in fancy saw, with cries of horror. How I would tax the keenest ingenuity of my childish mind—devising how in case the good God should permit the devil chief to appropriate me as his own, and take me to his place of torture—I might scale its sulphurous walls and free myself once more.

"Such was my life, and my terrible fears,
Like an angry cloud, darkning my earlier years.
Lest I fell to the pit, of which churchmen tell,
Which bears the horrific name of hell,
Far down in some hideous, gloomy place,
Where myriad crowds of the human race,
Were loudly groaning in deep despair,
Where burning brimstone obscures the air,
Where infernal shrieks ring loud and long,
And constitutes their eternal song."

These were the fears that continued to haunt me, until with the develodment of mind, reason assumed the helm and I was euabled to cast off my old belief in a Moloch for a God, and such a hell of torture for the soul with devils damned, and all the paraphanalia of terrorism which the church had imposed upon me. And when I was enabled to free myself from its vampire fangs which it had fastened deep within my soul, robbing me of much of the happiness which belongs to childhood, and was at last enabled through the evidences which the spiritual philosophy afforded, to accept its teachings which I received as truth—to embrace its hopes and feel assured by its promises, think you my friends, to use the expression of this terror inspiring priest, that I felt as if I had been robbed of any wholesome fear? Not at all. And I assure him that I will never bring an action against him should he steal from me all the old theology in which I had been trained, and the terrifying belief of my early years.

But lastly and above all other reasons I would give when asked, what is the use of spiritualism, and what benefits result from its teachings, is, that it is truth. I hold that no truth or fact in nature can be so insignificant as to be of no use to man. If it is truth, it is worthy of our study, and should be understood; and that the phenomena on which spiritualism is based, occur as is represented, and that their correct interpretation is such as has been rendered, I believe to be as well established and proven as that of any other occurrences in nature. It is the sum of truths, or knowledge of nature's infinite laws and modes of operation which we gain in our journey through life, by the patient study of which we are enabled to understand what before was mystery, that distinguishes the man intellectually from the child. It is the correct interpretation—application, of and harmonizing with them,—that goes to make up and perfect our moral nature; and every item we glean from the realm of truth, we should treasure as a gem of too much value to be lost. In this utilitarian age the question, What is its use? meets us at every turn in life—particularly is it proffered by those who regard everything as useless and aimless, which does not minister to their prejudices or satisfy their mercenary cravings. Too often with them its use depends upon whether it will bring gold. To such I would reply, yes, *Gold*, precious gold, and also bread. For every truth you gather enriches the mind and is food which adds to your intellectual growth.

Do you know why the world has spent its thousands of treasure and sacrificed so many valuable lives in its search in the polar seas? Was it for the dollars and cents they would receive in return? I reply, no; but it was to gather a few more items in regard to our physical geography, and solve a few more scientific problems, and thus increase the sum of human knowledge. Can you tell me why the astronomer, and men of science, will spend years of toil in studying those starry worlds whose distance from us is so great that a knowledge of them can have but little connection with the practical affairs of life? Why they labor to measure their almost incomprehensible distances when a measuring line equalizing the breadth of the earth's orbit would be doubled almost to infinity; why they engage in such long and tiresome vigils to unravel the mysteries of their movements; why so eager to obtain a knowledge of their physical condition, of the laws which govern, and the elements which enter into their composition, to learn of the sodium and potassum existing in the sun, or of the iron and the hydrogen entering into the composition of the star or nebula? Is it for wealth that he thus toils? Aye, for wealth, I say; wealth such as paltry gold cannot procure; wealth which enriches the world; wealth which adds to his value as a man, and which he will carry with him in his journey to the skies.

Can you tell me why the naturalist is willing to spend years in the study of a feeble insect, in learning the domestic habits of the bee, or ant, in studying the anatomy of the worm, and numbering the teeth of the snail? Why each flower and leaf which springs by the wayside, no matter how humble, is not considered too insignificant, for him to devote years of study to in order to gain a more complete knowledge of them? Is it for gain that he does this? Yes, it is for gain, such as death cannot deprive him of, and such as he shall know to be true riches when he meets the miser of earth beyond life's flood, stripped of the false wealth he had hoarded here.

And if these things of comparative insignificance are considered worthy long years of patient toil and study, think you not spiritualism, or the science of the soul, which proves to man his immortality—which informs him of his destiny and gives him a more perfect knowledge of himself and of the nature of the soul and its mysterious workings—is a benefit and of use; which teaches him his duties and relations to the world of spirits unseen, incarcerated within the flesh, (and whom he recognizes only through the corporeal masks they wear,) as well as his relation to the spirit world, equally near, but which—having dropped their grosser material covering—he no longer perceives through the organs of sense which belong to his physical nature? Do you not regard this as a subject of sufficient benefit and importance to man to claim a portion of his study and attention? And does it not show a profound ignorance on the part of those who ask the question, of what benefit is spiritualism to man? But were there no other answer than that already given to this question, *viz.*: That it is truth, it would be all-sufficient; for truth will never fail to lead us aright, and we should ever be most earnest in its pursuit. Nor can I more fully give expression to this sentiment than by a quotation from one of the beautiful poems of Mrs. Tappan:

Flow on thou river of truth,
  Past priests and temples of men,
Where the children of earth have been chained,
  In the darkness of error's deep den.
Thou wilt soon undermine all the walls,
  Thou wilt bring the temples all down,
And then on thy bosom wilt bear
  The bright sunshine, not errors deep frown,
Oh, beautiful river of truth.

Flow on thou beautiful stream,
  Through the valley and shadow of death;
That dreadful and desolate dream,
  Haunting men in their every breath;
Staring them in the face like a ghosr,
  A gloomy, weird ghost of the past,
Flow on to the beautiful coast,
  Where terror nor darkness can last,
Oh, wondrous river of truth.

And at last, O river of truth,
  Out into eternity's sea,
All laden with smiles and with tears,
  And the hopes of humanity;
Thou shalt roll with thy white pinioned sails,
  The sails of thine own angel throng;
And these shall float up in the gales
  That to bright golden regions belong.
And thou shall be merged in the sea
And the souls of all men merged in thee,
  Oh, beautiful river of truth.

And thus I hope I have to some extent given a satisfactory reply, as I have compared the religion of the past with the philosophy of spiritualism, which has it foundation in those inspirational teachings received through mediumistic channels from our friends in spirit life, which are remarkable for their unity of sentiment, and above all for coinciding with what our reason and judgment tell us is truth, without which we could not accept them.

Old theology teaches that punishment for sin is the infliction of the arbitrary judgment rendered in heaven's high chancery to satisfy the wrath of an offended God for errors committed in this life, and that man, though practicing wickedness up to the latest hour of a long life, yet if previous to death he should but believe in the man Christ as his savior, and that he was the eternal God, and be baptised, and is considered requisite also by others, repent that he had committed sin, that immediately a state of complete moral purity results and perfect exemption from retribution follows.

On the contrary, spiritualism teaches that suffering is the legitimate and inevitable result of the transgression of the physical or moral laws,—that corruption cannot at once be changed to purity, but that goodness with its offspring happiness is of slow growth and the result of the labor of a life.

Think you not the world is better for that system of moral philosophy we have embraced, which teaches that man is always responsible for his acts, and that punishment for wrong is inevitable, following as a natura consequence, and not as an arbitrary decree, and from which there is no escape, presenting therefore the greatest motive for men to live uprightly, and that happiness, which is the aim and object of every effort we put forth, is the necessary and certain reward of a life of purity and goodness —of cultivating the higher elements of our humanity—of living in conformity and harmonizing with all the physical, intellectual and moral laws with which we are brought in relation; that we can never shift the responsibility of our acts upon another who is innocent of them; but that the soul becomes bright and beautiful, or dark and loathsome, as each one weaves for himself his web of life in which he becomes clothed as in a garment. Think you not, my friends, that the world is far better for entertaining a belief this, which harmonizes with reason, and of which the judgment approves, rather than in a code of morals which teaches man that morality and goodness will not save him from punishment; that a man may live in violation of all God's laws, defying every requirement of truth, justice, and right, and at the termination of a long life of wickedness, by a metaphysical dodge, if I may so expsess it, escape all retribution and be at once transformed into an angel of purity and light?

And thus I hope I have satisfactorily answered the question, Of what benefit is spiritualism to man?; and given you sufficient reasons why mankind individually and collectively are happier and better for its teachings, and for the truths which it reveals; and I trust I have been able to answer it in such a manner as no reasonable mind will fail to appreciate. But I could not expect to satisfy all; as there is a class of mind so constituted that they obstinately shut their eyes towards everything which conflicts with their prejudices, whom no reasoning would convince, as they have determined that no argument except it favors their own views shall have any weight with them. To such minds it is useless to present facts or reasons, as they would not believe "though one rose from the dead." We believe that we are pursueing the truth, and you may be sure that the truth will always benefit us. We believe that mind here is receiving that training which will prove of vast benefit to it, and will materially advance its progress in its journey through the spheres, that the future life is to be one of intellectual activity and progress, that we, with all else in nature are advancing, and that we will through all coming time continue to mount higher and still higher in the intellectual and moral scale, and as the infinite years in ceaseless cycles revolve and the onward and ever onward stream of time bears us into the boundless future, the soul will continue to gather fresh lessons of wisdom, to reap new harvests of truth and consequent happiness from the unexplored universe before us.

Mind will never cease to find material on which to feed, for it can neither comprehend infinity nor fathom all truth; for the laws of nature, which are those of God, are as infinite in number, and the modes of their application, as it is possible to arrange the combinations of matter. And what imagination is there so bold as to predict the wondrous height which mind may reach, or what powers it may attain in the ages yet to come, while studying the infinite plan of creation, it shall roam through the universe of God, learning of the wondrous laws which guide and sustain the worlds whose numbers perhaps sprinkle all space, which is infinite; and how trifling will then appear the petty annoyances which disturb us now. The prospects in the great and glorious future which awaits us, where we may hope for an eternal union of hearts which have left us behind in the flight to the bright and beautiful land, should lead us to take a broad and comprehensive view of life and its duties, and bear with cheerfulness that separation of earthly ties which is but for a moment, and is common to all men in this lower sphere of existence.

"And thus through our boats on the sea of life,
Together may drift in their musical chime,
Or be driven apart by the waves of strife,
And the winds that beat from the shores of time;
Yet 'tis sweet to think that no storms can sever
The immortal heirs of a bright forever.

"Swift are the life tides drifting us on,
Soon we shall stand on the beautiful shore,
In the morn of a life whose night shall not come,
In the dawn of a day that shall never be o'er;
Oh, wealth of the ages and joy of the spheres,
Ye shall crown us at last with the glory of years."

www.ingramcontent.com/pod-product-compliance
Lightning Source LLC
LaVergne TN
LVHW010743120826
845150LV00009B/2281